IS THAT A FACT?

Does It Really Take Seven Years to Digest Swallowed Gum?

And Other Questions You've Always Wanted to Ask

SANDY DONOVAN

ILLUSTRATIONS BY COLIN W. THOMPSON

LERNER PUBLICATIONS COMPANY

Minneapolis

Contents

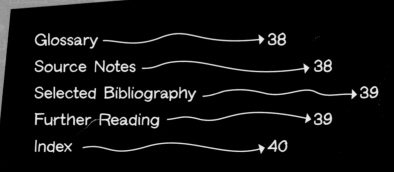

Perhaps you've heard these common sayings about familiar items and everyday events:

A penny placed on a train track can cause a train to derail! Water boiled in a microwave can suddenly "explode"!

But are these sayings true? Is there any science behind the stories? Come along with us as we explore these old beliefs and more. Find out whether the stories and sayings you hear every day are **FACT** OR **FICTION!**

When You Bite on a Wint-O-Green Life Saver in the Dark, Does It Make a Spark?

YES! It's actually the act of teeth biting on the sugar in Life Savers that makes the spark. Scientists have known about this for centuries. In 1620 the scientist Francis Bacon wrote, "It is . . . most certain that all sugar . . . sparkles when broken or scraped with a knife in the dark."

Later, another scientist discussed how this discovery could be used for pulling practical jokes. Giambattista Beccaria wrote in 1753, "You may, when in the dark, frighten . . . people only by chewing lumps of sugar, and, in the meantime, keeping your mouth open, which will appear to them as if full of fire."

You may be wondering, then, why we see sparks only from Wint-O-Green Life Savers and not all sugary candy. Actually, Beccaria was slightly exaggerating the effect. All sugar does produce a spark when chewed. But this spark is ultraviolet light. And that's invisible to the human eye. Wint-O-Green Life Savers contain an ingredient that turns ultraviolet light into blue green light, which we can see. The ingredient is the oil of wintergreen that flavors them.

Can You Fry an Egg on the Sidewalk If It's Very Warm Outside?

SORT OF. But you'd need a little help from something besides the sun. To cook an egg, you need pretty high heat. The white of an egg turns solid between 144 and 149°F (62 and 65°C). The yolk needs a little higher temperature: between 149 and 158°F (65 and 70°C).

On a very hot day, the outside temperature might reach 110°F (43°C). But even then, a sidewalk wouldn't get hot enough to cook an egg. Concrete—the material usually used to make sidewalks—gets hot in the sun. But it doesn't get *that* hot.

Still, there are some tricks you can use to cook an egg on a sidewalk. Materials such as metal and glass conduct heat. That means heat moves through them—and they get hotter. You could hold a piece of glass or metal over your egg. Try a magnifying glass or a mirror. If you hold the glass at the right angle, you can catch some of the sun's heat and conduct it over your egg. But one warning: as the American Egg Board cautions, "Sidewalks are not very clean. So, if you see someone try to fry an egg on the sidewalk, don't eat the egg!"

Did You Know?
Oatman, Arizona, hosts a sidewalk egg-frying contest every Fourth of July. The only rule is that you can't use any heat other than that of the sun to fry your egg. People fry plenty of eggs that day. But they get help from mirrors, magnifying glasses, and even solar-powered (sun-powered) ovens.

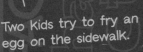
Two kids try to fry an egg on the sidewalk.

Can You Fly If You Tie Enough Helium-Filled Balloons to You?

YES. But you'd probably need special balloons. Any helium-filled balloon can carry an object through the air. However, it would take a lot of regular-sized helium balloons to carry you. (Try the activity on page 9 to find out just how many.)

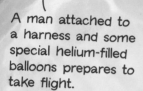
A man attached to a harness and some special helium-filled balloons prepares to take flight.

An easier way to fly is to use extra-large balloons. Some people have successfully flown by tying such balloons to themselves. The balloons are between 4 and 7 feet (1 and 2 meters) tall. They are normally used for advertising, or drawing people's attention to items that are for sale. The sport of flying with advertising balloons even has a name: cluster ballooning.

In cluster ballooning, a person wears a harness with a bunch of the big balloons attached to it. The person has to be tethered, or tied, to something on the ground while the clusters of balloons are tied to him or her. When all the balloons are in place, the person is untied—and he or she takes off! To come down, the person cuts off a few balloons at a time until he or she begins to descend. (Of course, the person also carries an emergency parachute, just in case.)

Try This!

How many regular-sized helium balloons would you need to fly? Find out by blowing up one balloon and attaching paper clips to the balloon's string. Attach the clips one by one until you've added enough to hold the balloon down. Count the number of clips, and multiply that number by the weight of one clip (about 0.01 ounces, or 0.3 grams). You've figured how much weight one single balloon can carry. Now weigh yourself to see how many balloons you'd need.

Is It Possible to Swing 360 Degrees on a Swing Set?

You may have heard this common legend on the playground: if you pump your legs fast enough, you can make your swing go over the top of the swing set and down around the back to complete a full circle. **BUT IT ISN'T TRUE.**

10

Two things make this feat impossible. One is gravity (the force that pulls objects toward the surface of Earth). The second is the swing itself and the pliable, or bendable, chains or ropes that connect it to the swing set bar. Once you swing past 90 degrees, or a quarter of a circle, gravity begins to kick in. This means that the swing is getting pulled toward Earth even as it continues on its circle. The force of the swing's movement may win out for a while past 90 degrees, and the swing will continue on its circle journey. But once it begins to reach 180 degrees—half a circle— gravity will begin to win. At this point,

the flexible ropes or chains bend and allow the swing to fall down toward Earth—or the swing set bar (ouch!).

The only way for a swing to make it the full 360 degrees is for the force of the swing's movement to be greater than the force of gravity. Nobody has proved this is possible on a regular playground swing. But people have used some tricks to make a swing go in a full circle. One of these is to use boards to connect the swing to the bar. With boards instead of chains or ropes, the force needed to resist gravity is less. Another trick is to use something to beef up the swing's force. In one experiment, a TV crew strapped a rocket to a dummy on a swing. With help from rocket power, the swing was able to overcome gravity's pull. Of course, strapping a rocket to yourself at the playground is not recommended.

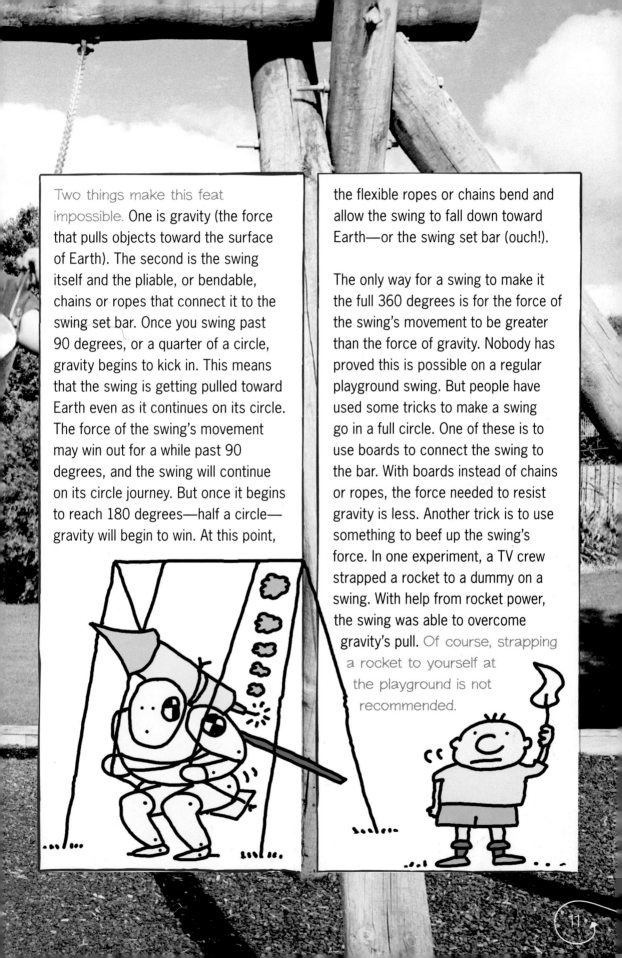

Does the Average Human Consume Four Spiders per Year While Sleeping?

NO! In fact, it's unlikely that a spider would let itself get swallowed by a person. To get swallowed, a spider would have to climb or fall into a person's mouth. And a spider's sense of self-preservation—its will to live—would keep it from climbing in.

If a spider happened to crawl near a sleeping human's mouth, the spider would hear breathing. To a spider, that's the sound of an enemy. Its instinct would be to flee, not to climb in.

Baby spiders float through the air when they first hatch—but even floating baby spiders almost never get swallowed by people!

But could a spider fall into a sleeping person's mouth? Not likely. Adult spiders just don't fall that often. However—and maybe this is where the myth comes from—baby spiders do fall, or float, through the air when they hatch out of their egg sac. In fact, when one spider egg sac hatches, hundreds of too-small-to-see baby spiders get thrown into the air. They "ride" the air current to wherever they land.

Sure, some of these baby spiders might land in the mouth of a sleeping person. And they might get swallowed. But the chance of an egg sac happening to hatch near a sleeping person is pretty slim. And the chance of the sleeping person's mouth being open and facing upward isn't all that great either. So, while it's *possible*, it's highly unlikely that the average person swallows four spiders per year. Plus, does it count if the spider is too small to see?

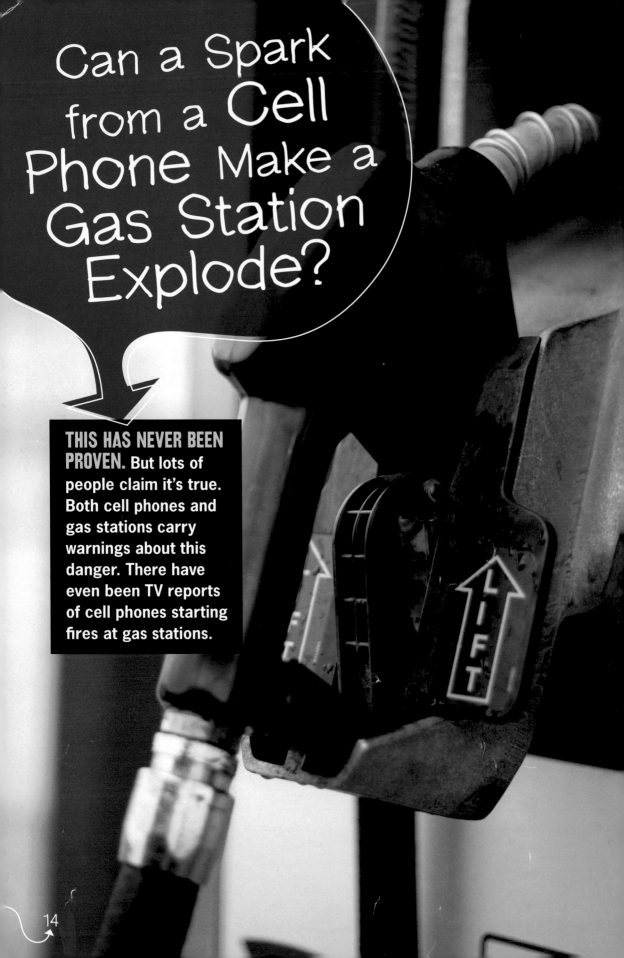

Can a Spark from a Cell Phone Make a Gas Station Explode?

THIS HAS NEVER BEEN PROVEN. But lots of people claim it's true. Both cell phones and gas stations carry warnings about this danger. There have even been TV reports of cell phones starting fires at gas stations.

Factoid

<u>Static electricity caused by people's clothes rubbing against the sides of their cars can cause a gas station fire. For this reason, people should not get back into their cars while gas is pumping into their fuel tank.</u>

One story came out of New Paltz, New York, in 2004. TV stations reported that flames burst out around a twenty-one-year-old college student whose cell phone rang as he was pumping gas. "Firefighters believe the cell phone ignited vapors coming from the car's fuel tank as it was being filled," CBS News reported.

The claim is that the batteries used in cell phones can ignite the gas fumes while gas is being pumped into a car. But the fire chief in New Paltz later said that this story was not true. After further investigation, he found that the cell phone was not the source of the fire.

In fact, the batteries used in cell phones are the same voltage (electrical power) as car batteries. And cell phone batteries deliver much less of that power at any one time than car batteries do.

Does It Really Take Seven Years to Digest Swallowed Gum?

NO! Gum is odd stuff indeed. Even after you've chewed on it for hours, it remains basically unchanged. Anything else would be reduced to nothing after only a few minutes of chewing. But gum just keeps on going.

This X-ray shows the stomach and intestines of a person. Could gum sit around in there for seven years? No!

So you might think it makes sense to believe that it would take years for our digestive systems to break gum down. In fact, gum never gets broken down in our stomachs as other foods do. That's why it's often called indigestible. But just because it doesn't get digested doesn't mean it stays around in our stomachs for years. Gum travels through our digestive system just as fast as anything else. Usually that's in less than twenty-four hours.

Gum has one special ingredient that makes it indigestible. It's called gum base. That's a rubbery substance that is found in the sap of some trees. It can also be human-made. Either way, it's rubbery stuff that you can chew on for hours. Gum also has a little vegetable oil to keep it soft, a little glycerin to keep it moist, and sugar or corn syrup to make it sweet. (Sugarless gum has artificial sweetener instead of sugar.)

The first chewing gum was made in the 1800s. But people chewed on tree sap even before gum was invented. In fact, scientists believe many ancient peoples chewed sap from trees. Maybe their mothers told them not to swallow it or it would stay in their stomachs for seven years!

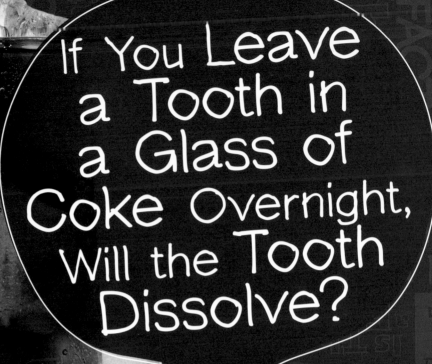

If You Leave a Tooth in a Glass of Coke Overnight, Will the Tooth Dissolve?

NOPE. You may have heard stories about this. Some stories even claim there's scientific proof that Coke makes teeth dissolve. The stories say that scientists left something overnight in a glass of Coke. The object is sometimes a baby tooth or a penny or even a dead fly. And when the scientists checked in the morning, the tooth—or the penny or the dead fly—was gone! If Coke can do that to a tooth—or a penny or a fly—imagine what it can do to your stomach! At least, that's what people who tell these stories say.

But while there are plenty of tales about Coke dissolving things, there's never been any real proof that it could happen. In fact, Coke can't dissolve anything overnight. It's true that sodas contain some pretty harsh ingredients. For instance, they are full of citric acid. And citric acid would eventually dissolve a tooth (after a couple of weeks or more of soaking). But other, more healthful drinks contain citric acid too. There's a lot of it in orange juice. And no one worries about orange juice dissolving teeth! Besides, when you drink a beverage, it passes over your teeth pretty quickly.

You don't usually hold it in your mouth for any length of time. If you tried, you could probably hold it in your mouth for a few minutes. Or maybe even half an hour if you're really dedicated. But a couple of weeks? Probably not.

Try This!

Do your own experiment. Fill three glasses with different fluids. You might try Coke, orange juice, and water. Then let three identical objects soak in the glasses overnight. Try three pennies or perhaps three pieces of chalk. In the morning, check to see if any of the fluids changed the objects in any way.

Can Reusing Plastic Water Bottles Cause Cancer?

NO. But this myth has been repeated so often that many people believe it. According to the rumor, water bottles are made out of a substance called DEHA. Rinsing and reusing the bottles can supposedly cause them to break down. When this happens, DEHA can leak into the beverage. And when you drink it, you can get cancer.

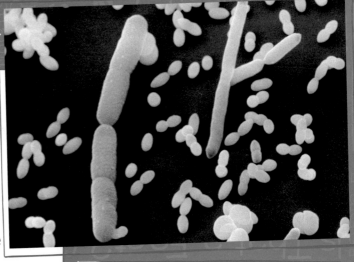

Bacteria like this can grow in used plastic water bottles.

In fact, DEHA isn't even an ingredient in plastic water bottles. And even if it were, no evidence shows that it causes cancer. In the United States, the U.S. Food and Drug Administration makes sure that all food and beverage packaging is safe. The Food and Drug Administration has found that the plastic used for water bottles is safe. This means the bottles are safe to use over and over.

But even though it won't cause cancer, reusing plastic water bottles is not a good idea. It can make you sick—not from any cancer-causing ingredients but from bacteria. Bacteria are microscopic living things that exist all around us. Bacteria don't always hurt people. But some bacteria can make you sick.

The bacteria that live in used water bottles carry germs from people's mouths. These germs can cause severe stomach infections. If you absolutely must reuse, make sure you wash out the bottle with warm, soapy water. And dry it thoroughly! Bacteria love to grow in warm, moist areas.

To Use or Not to Use

Plastic water bottles are safe for humans. But they hurt the planet. Many of them are not recycled. And shipping bottled water to stores causes pollution. Buying one good reusable bottle and filling it with tap water may not be a bad idea!

Can You Get Free Items by Pouring Salt Water into Vending Machine Coin Slots?

THIS USED TO BE TRUE. But thanks to smart vending machine companies, this trick no longer works.

In the mid-1990s, there were lots of reports of people pouring salt water into vending machine coin slots. This caused the coin changers to short-circuit. The result was often free products like sodas or candy. Sometimes the machines even spit out extra money. Of course, another result was trouble. This prank was illegal. It caused huge damage to the vending machines. Still, it happened pretty often, especially at college campuses. Lots of people got in trouble with their schools or with the police. Then it began to spread to other countries. In places such as Great Britain, vending machine coin slots are quite large. That's because some coins are bigger in Great Britain. Pouring salt water

down these coin slots caused even more expensive damage than in the United States.

So vending machine companies took action. They invented machines that stand up to salt water. They moved the coin changer to different spots in the machines. This made it harder for salt water to travel to the changer and short-circuit it. These days, almost no machines remain that can be short-circuited by salt water.

Companies have improved vending machines—so pouring salt water into them doesn't mean free food or drinks.

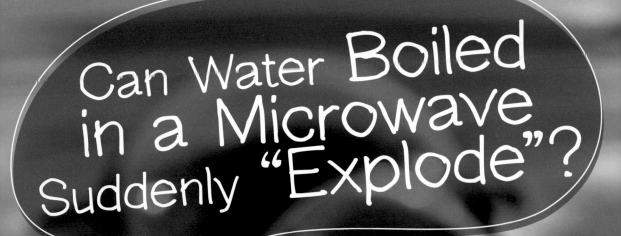

Can Water Boiled in a Microwave Suddenly "Explode"?

IT'S POSSIBLE. But it's very unlikely. In fact, there's a word for what happens to liquid that gets too hot in a microwave. It's called superheating. Superheating is when liquid reaches a higher temperature than what it needs to boil.

Usually water boils at 212°F (100°C). Then tiny bubbles form on the surface and help to cool the water. They keep the water's temperature from rising much above 212°F. But in a microwave, water can get hotter than 212°F without boiling. This can happen only if the water is heated in a completely smooth glass or cup. And there can't be anything else in the cup, such as a drink mix or a spoon.

Hot water needs something to "trigger" its boiling. On a stove, the hot metal pot or kettle triggers boiling. But in a microwave, the cup or glass

does not get hot as the water heats up. A little drink mix or a wooden stir stick would serve as a trigger. Without anything like that in the cup, the water is just waiting for an outside trigger to come along and help it boil. But by this time, it is so hot that instead of boiling, it may actually explode. This has happened when people added cocoa mix to a cup of heated water. It has even happened when they just slightly moved the cup. The water can explode simply by being sloshed up on the side of the cup.

Don't Try This at Home!

The risk of superheating water is low. But the consequences can be extreme. Exploding water can cause severe burns on your face or body. Just to be safe, always place a stir stick or other object in a cup you are heating in the microwave. Just be sure the object you choose isn't metal. Metal should not be microwaved.

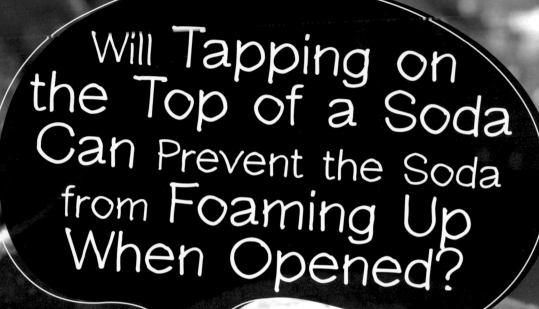

Will Tapping on the Top of a Soda Can Prevent the Soda from Foaming Up When Opened?

NO! There is one ingredient in soda that causes it to foam. It's a gas called carbon dioxide. Soda is made by adding carbon dioxide to water under high pressure. Pressure is the force produced when air presses on water. And when a soda can is sealed shut, the pressure inside the can remains high.

But when the can is opened, the pressure drops quickly. The air that was pressing on the liquid inside the can escapes from the can. This causes little bubbles of carbon dioxide to form in the liquid. They rise quickly to the surface of the drink. There they form many tiny bubbles that turn into fizz.

Shaking a can before you open it will make even more foam. Why? Because shaking makes the carbon dioxide start to separate from the liquid while it's still sealed inside the can. And then when you open it, even more bubbles are just waiting to break free.

So can you make the carbon dioxide bubbles go back down into the liquid by tapping on the top of the can before you open it? Nope. The only thing that will help is time. If you wait long enough, the carbon dioxide will mix itself back in with the drink. So if it seems as if tapping the can prevents a big foam up, it may be because of the time it took to do the tapping.

Tapping the top of a soda can before you open it does not stop the soda in the can from foaming up.

Is There a Special Chemical That Can Detect Urine in a Swimming Pool?

Don't believe anyone who tells you that a pool has a magic pee-sensing chemical. You may have heard this rumor about public pools, school pools, or someone's private pool. Kids are warned that if they pee in the pool, the chemical will sense the urine and turn the surrounding water red. Or purple. Or bright orange. **WHATEVER THE COLOR, IT'S NOT TRUE. THE CHEMICAL DOESN'T EXIST.**

Signs like this are meant to keep people from using pools as a bathroom.

Welcome
To Our
OOL
NOTICE THERE IS
NO "P" IN IT
LET'S KEEP IT THAT WAY.

Scientists say they could invent such a chemical. But it would be hard to limit the false alarms. A false alarm would be when a substance similar to pee triggered the colorful reaction. For example, sweat has many of the same ingredients as pee. And it would be hard to keep sweaty bodies out of a swimming pool.

Pool suppliers say they get plenty of requests for the "pee-sensing dye." But, they say, it's probably best that there's no such thing. After all, if there really were such a chemical, what kid would be able to resist testing it out? Wouldn't *you* be tempted to see those brightly colored trails in the water? You could always blame it on your little brother or another kid swimming by, right?

Is the Number of People Alive Today Greater Than the Number Who Have Ever Died?

NO A lot of people use this "fact" as an example of how huge the world's population is. And the world's population *is* huge—and growing. Of course, any estimate of the current world population is just that—an estimate. Scientists look at things such as surveys, statistics, and data on different countries. Then they do some math to estimate world population. No one can really know *exactly* how many people are living at one given time.

The U.S. Census Bureau—an organization that provides information on populations—estimates that on July 1, 2009, there were about 6.7 billion people alive. And they estimate that on July 1, 2019, there will be nearly 7.5 billion people alive. That's almost 800 million more people in ten years! That's a big jump in world population in just one decade. It almost makes sense to think that there would be more people alive today than the total of all people who ever lived. But a few simple checks show that that's impossible.

Estimating the total number of people who have ever lived is tricky. The answer can change depending on when you begin counting. Some people believe modern humans have existed for about 40,000 years. Estimates of how many people have lived since then range between about 45 billion and 125 billion. One scientist did a very complicated set of math equations and got the number 106,456,367,669 as the total number of humans who ever lived. That would mean that today's 6.7 billion people are only about 6 percent of the people who have ever died. That's a lot less than the "fact" above claims.

India is one of the most populous countries in the world.

Will Eggs Really Stand on Their Ends during the Vernal Equinox?

The vernal equinox is the first day of spring. It is one of two days in the year when day and night last exactly the same length of time. It comes on about March 21. **AND EGGS REALLY *WILL* STAND ON THEIR ENDS DURING THIS TIME!** But they'll also stand on their ends on any other day of the year.

Go ahead and amaze your friends and family. Gather them together around March 21. Then demonstrate how you can stand an egg on end. Just don't let them know that you could do the same thing on any other day.

Eggs represent spring in many countries—including the United States, where some people put eggs in baskets, and in China, where people dye eggs red.

The rumor about the vernal equinox has been around for centuries. People think it began in ancient China, where folks celebrated the first day of spring by balancing eggs. The demonstration was said to show that all of nature was in balance on that day. But somewhere along the way, the ancient

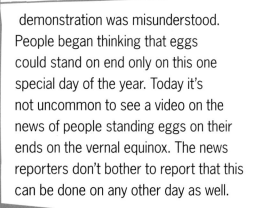

demonstration was misunderstood. People began thinking that eggs could stand on end only on this one special day of the year. Today it's not uncommon to see a video on the news of people standing eggs on their ends on the vernal equinox. The news reporters don't bother to report that this can be done on any other day as well.

Try This!

Do your own experiment to see if you can get eggs to balance. It doesn't always work the first time, so keep practicing. Test it in warm weather and cold weather. Try it with warm eggs and cold eggs. You can also try it with eggs of different sizes. What can you discover?

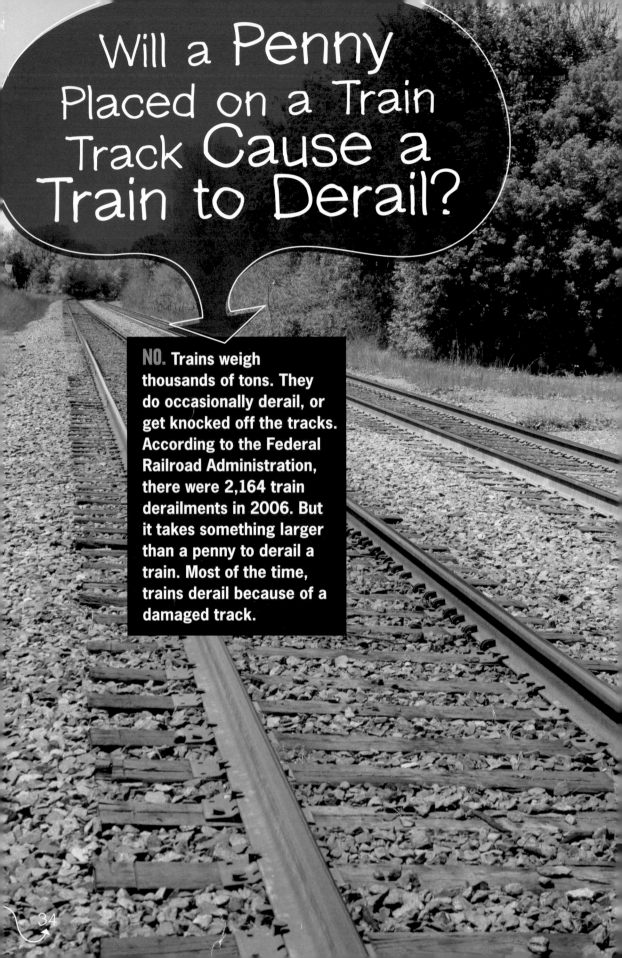

Will a Penny Placed on a Train Track Cause a Train to Derail?

NO. Trains weigh thousands of tons. They do occasionally derail, or get knocked off the tracks. According to the Federal Railroad Administration, there were 2,164 train derailments in 2006. But it takes something larger than a penny to derail a train. Most of the time, trains derail because of a damaged track.

You will get one result from placing a penny on a train track. You'll get a squished penny. Since trains were invented, people have been fascinated by this result. Some people collect pennies that have been smashed by different trains. But don't try it yourself. At least four people have died trying to flatten pennies under trains. Some of them didn't get out of the way on time. Others were standing on one track waiting for a train to come down the other track. They didn't know that a train was approaching from behind them on the track they were standing on!

Factoid

Even though you won't derail a train, trying to place a penny on a train track is not a good idea. You are not only in danger of getting squashed yourself. You or someone else could get seriously hurt if the penny flew out from under the train's wheels.

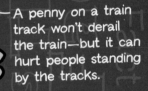

A penny on a train track won't derail the train—but it can hurt people standing by the tracks.

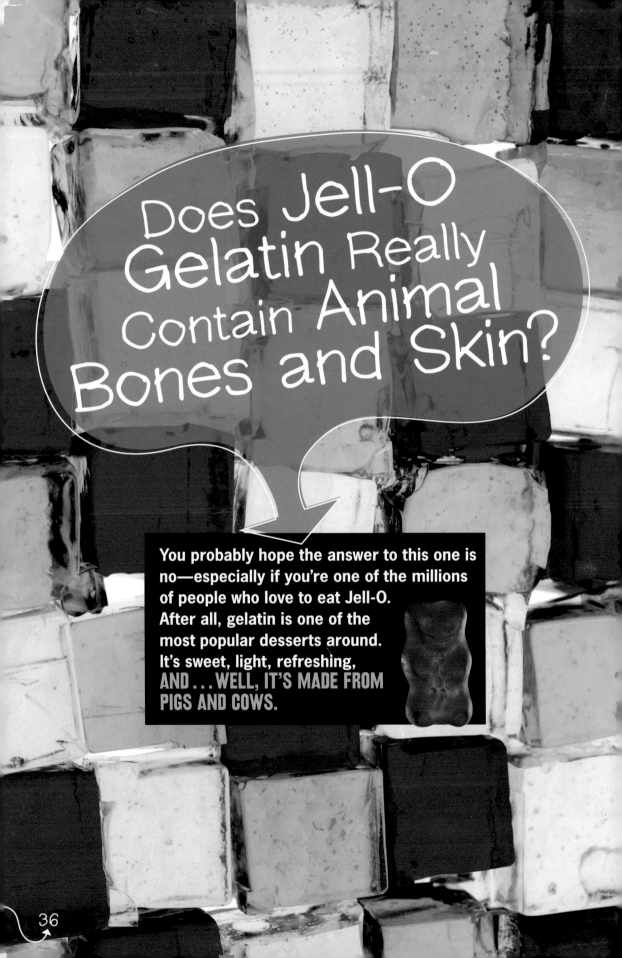

Does Jell-O Gelatin Really Contain Animal Bones and Skin?

You probably hope the answer to this one is no—especially if you're one of the millions of people who love to eat Jell-O. After all, gelatin is one of the most popular desserts around. It's sweet, light, refreshing, AND...WELL, IT'S MADE FROM PIGS AND COWS.

Yep—it's true! To make gelatin, you need collagen—a tough, gluelike protein found in vertebrates (animals with backbones). To get collagen, people extract it—or remove it—from the bones, skins, and hides of animals. They usually use pigs and cows. Then they boil the collagen in water or acid and grind it into a dry powder.

Another common belief, that Jell-O is made of animal hooves, is *not* true. Hooves don't have enough collagen to turn them into Jell-O. So that's a relief, right? But for many people, the bones and skins are enough to turn them off from Jell-O. Many vegetarians, in particular, refuse to eat Jell-O or any gelatin-based products. Still, the shiny, jiggly treat is well loved by many. It's served not just as dessert but in salads and main courses too.

Jell-O isn't the only gelatin-based food. Many other popular treats—such as gummy bears and some fruit snacks—also contain gelatin.

Did You Know?

There's a Jell-O museum in LeRoy, New York—the city where Jell-O was created. At the museum, you can learn about the history of Jell-O. You can also see Jell-O artwork created by such famous artists as Norman Rockwell.

GLOSSARY

bacteria: microscopic living things that exist all around us and inside us

cancer: a disease in which some cells in the body grow faster than normal cells and destroy healthy organs and tissues

carbon dioxide: a gas that is a mixture of carbon and oxygen and has no color or odor

citric acid: a substance found in citrus fruits, such as lemons and limes. Citric acid is often used to flavor soda.

collagen: a tough, gluelike protein found in animals with backbones

conduct: to transfer heat or electricity through an object

gelatin: a clear substance used in making desserts and jelly that is obtained from animal bones and skin

glycerin: a sweet, colorless, thick liquid used in gum and soap

gravity: the force that pulls objects toward the surface of Earth

indigestible: not able to be digested

pliable: bendable

sap: the liquid that flows through a plant, carrying water and food from one part of the plant to another

superheat: to heat a liquid at a higher temperature than what it needs to boil

ultraviolet light: light that is invisible to the human eye

vegetarian: a person who does not eat meat

vernal equinox: the first day of spring. The vernal equinox is one of two days in the year when the day and night last exactly the same length of time.

vertebrate: an animal with a backbone

SOURCE NOTES

5 Francis Bacon, quoted in Kenneth Chang, "Sweet Spark May Hold Clue to How Things Break," *New York Times*, June 19, 2007, http://www.nytimes.com/2007/06/19/science/19winto.html (March 9, 2009).

5 Giambattista Beccaria, quoted in Kenneth Chang, "Sweet Spark May Hold Clue to How Things Break," *New York Times*, June 19, 2007, http://www.nytimes.com/2007/06/19/science/19winto.html (March 9, 2009).

7 American Egg Board, "Answers to AEB's Fascinating Egg Facts Game," *Aeb.org*, n.d., http://www.aeb.org/KidsAndFamily/answers_to_fascinating_egg_facts.htm (March 9, 2009).

15 Lloyd de Vries, "Phone Ignites Gas Station Fire," *CBS News*, May 14, 2004, http://www.cbsnews.com/stories/2004/05/14/tech/main617547.shtml (March 11, 2009).

SELECTED BIBLIOGRAPHY

Chang, Kenneth. "Sweet Spark May Hold Clue to How Things Break." *New York Times,* June 19, 2007. http://www.nytimes.com/2007/06/19/science/19winto.html (March 9, 2009).

Engel, Peter H. *Old Wives Tales: The Truth about Everyday Myths.* New York: St. Martin's Press, 1993.

Haub, Carl. "How Many People Have Ever Lived on Earth?" *Population Today,* November–December 2002. Available online at Population Reference Bureau. 2009. http://www.prb.org/Articles/2002/HowManyPeopleHaveEverLivedonEarth.aspx (March 12, 2009).

O'Connor, Anahad. "The Claim: Swallowed Gum Takes a Long Time to Digest." *New York Times*, August 28, 2007. http://www.nytimes.com/2007/08/28/health/28real.html?_r=1&oref=slogin (March 12, 2009).

Urban Legends Reference Pages. *Snopes .com.* N.d. http://www.snopes.com (March 12, 2009).

FURTHER READING

American Folklore: Urban Legends http://www.americanfolklore.net/urban-legends.html This website features twenty well-known, spooky urban legends—those popular myths and stories about mysterious happenings and unexplained events.

Donovan, Sandy. *Does an Apple a Day Keep the Doctor Away?: And Other Questions about Your Health and Body.* Minneapolis: Lerner Publications Company, 2010. This fun title explores the truth behind common sayings and beliefs about health and the human body.

Everyday Mysteries http://www.loc.gov/rr/scitech/mysteries Check out this site to find the answers to other interesting questions you've always wanted to ask.

Kallen, Stuart A. *Urban Legends.* Farmington Hills, MI: Lucent Books, 2006. This in-depth book contains a wealth of information on urban legends.

Packard, Mary. *MythBusters: Don't Try This at Home!* San Francisco: Jossey-Bass, 2006. Come along with Adam Savage and Jamie Hyneman—stars of the popular Discovery Channel show *MythBusters*—as they examine fifteen fascinating myths.

Pascoe, Elaine. *Fooled You!: Fakes and Hoaxes Through the Years.* New York: Henry Holt, 2005. Learn the truth behind some outlandish stories and beliefs that have been spread throughout history.

Silverman, Buffy. *Can an Old Dog Learn New Tricks?: And Other Questions about Animals.* Minneapolis: Lerner Publications Company, 2010. Silverman reveals whether well-known sayings and beliefs about animals are true.

INDEX

ACKNOWLEDGMENTS
The images in this book are used with the permission of:
© Dave Bradley Photography/Taxi/Getty Images, pp. 1, 17 (bottom); © James Steidl/Dreamstime.com, pp. 2 (left), 18 (inset); © Todd Strand/Independent Picture Service, pp. 2 (right), 5, 22, 28 (inset); © Red2000/Dreamstime.com, pp. 3, 33 (bottom); © Sascha Burkard/Dreamstime.com, p. 4 (left); © Hartemink/Dreamstime.com, p. 4 (right); © iStockphoto.com/Patty Colabuono, p. 6; © Maxim Kulemza/Dreamstime.com, p. 7 (top left); © TimurD-Fotolia.com, p. 7 (top right); © Wave Royalty Free/Alamy, p. 7 (bottom); © Yuriy Panyukov/Dreamstime.com, pp. 8-9; © Louie Psihoyos/Science Faction/CORBIS, p. 9 (inset); © Wilfried Krecichwost/Digital Vision/Getty Images, pp. 10-11; © SW Productions/Photodisc/Getty Images, pp. 12-13; © Wayne Mckown/Dreamstime.com, p. 12 (inset); © Gary Retherford/Photo Researchers, Inc., p. 13 (inset); © Cwd/Dreamstime.com, p. 14; © Thesupe87/Dreamstime.com, p. 15 (top); © Glo5/Dreamstime.com, p. 15 (bottom); © Cusp/SuperStock, p. 16; © Bryan Mullennix/Photographer's Choice/Getty Images, p. 17 (top left); © SIU/Visuals Unlimited, Inc., p. 17 (top right); © Peterman-Fotolia.com, p. 18 (main); © Digital Vision/Getty Images, p. 19; © Gordon Galbraith/Dreamstime.com, p. 20; © David M. Phillips/Photo Researchers, Inc., p. 21 (top); © Peter Gudella/Dreamstime.com, p. 21 (bottom); © Flirt/SuperStock, p. 23 (top); © age fotostock/SuperStock, pp. 23 (bottom), 30 (inset); © Sergey Peterman/Dreamstime.com, pp. 24-25; © Marta Johnson, pp. 25 (left inset), 27 (inset), 34, 35 (right); © Kelpfish/Dreamstime.com, p. 25 (right inset); © Paul Reid/Dreamstime.com, pp. 26-27; © Dimitrii/Dreamstime.com, pp. 28-29; © Michal Miasko-Fotolia.com, p. 29 (inset); © Simon Bruty/Allsport/Getty Images, pp. 30-31; © Daniel Boiteau/Dreamstime.com, p. 31 (inset); © Jose Manuel Gelpi Diaz/Dreamstime.com, p. 32; © Edyta Pawlowska/Dreamstime.com, p. 33 (top left); © Keren Su/CORBIS, p. 33 (top right); © Sascha Burkard/Dreamstime.com, p. 35 (left); © Tracy Hebden/Dreamstime.com, p. 36 (main); © Magdalena Gieniusz-Fotolia.com, p. 36 (inset); © Laura Knox/Fresh Food Images/Photolibrary, p. 37 (top); © Kameleonmedia/Dreamstime.com, p. 37 (bottom).

Cover: © Dimitri Vervitsiotis/Digital Vision/Getty Images.

Copyright © 2010 by Sandy Donovan

Lerner Publications Company
A division of Lerner Publishing Group, Inc.
241 First Avenue North
Minneapolis, MN 55401 U.S.A.

Website address: www.lernerbooks.com

Library of Congress Cataloging-in-Publication Data

Donovan, Sandra, 1967–
    Does it really take seven years to digest swallowed gum? : and other questions you've always wanted to ask / by Sandy Donovan ; illustrated by Colin W. Thompson.
        p.   cm. — (Is that a fact?)
    Includes bibliographical references and index.
    ISBN 978-0-8225-9085-9 (lib. bdg. : alk. paper)
    Medicine—Miscellaneous—Juvenile literature.
I Thompson, Colin W., ill. II. Title.
R706.D66 2010
610—dc22   2009010642

Manufactured in the United States of America
1 – JR – 12/15/09